Pennsylvania Wildcats

"FRANCE" HOWER (1847-1915):
His faithful dog and two bobcats from Jack's Mountain.

PENNSYLVANIA WILD CATS

BY

HENRY W. SHOEMAKER

(Author of *The Pennsylvania Lion, or Panther*)

The patch is kind enough, but a huge feeder.
Snail-slow in profit, and he sleeps by day
More than the wild cat. —Shakespeare.

an imprint of Sunbury Press, Inc.
Mechanicsburg, PA USA

an imprint of Sunbury Press, Inc.
Mechanicsburg, PA USA

Copyright © 1916, 2025 by Henry W. Shoemaker.
Cover Copyright © 2024 by Sunbury Press, Inc.

Sunbury Press supports copyright. Copyright fuels creativity, encourages diverse voices, promotes free speech, and creates a vibrant culture. Thank you for buying an authorized edition of this book and for complying with copyright laws. Except for the quotation of short passages for the purpose of criticism and review, no part of this publication may be reproduced, scanned, or distributed in any form without permission. You are supporting writers and allowing Sunbury Press to continue to publish books for every reader. For information contact Sunbury Press, Inc., Subsidiary Rights Dept., PO Box 548, Boiling Springs, PA 17007 USA or legal@sunburypress.com.

For information about special discounts for bulk purchases, please contact Sunbury Press Orders Dept. at (855) 338-8359 or orders@sunburypress.com.

To request one of our authors for speaking engagements or book signings, please contact Sunbury Press Publicity Dept. at publicity@sunburypress.com.

FIRST CATAMOUNT PRESS EDITION: April 2025

Set in Adobe Garamond | Interior design by Crystal Devine | Cover by Lawrence Knorr | Foreword by Lawrence Knorr, Edited by Lawrence Knorr and Debra Reynolds, Annotated by Lawrence Knorr.

Publisher's Cataloging-in-Publication Data
Names: Shoemaker, Henry W., author.
Title: Pennsylvania wild cats / Henry W. Shoemaker.
Description: First trade paperback edition. | Mechanicsburg, PA : Catamount Press, 2025.
Summary: Henry Wharton Shoemaker details the various wild cats native to Pennsylvania and the men who hunted them in the 19th century.
Identifiers: ISBN : 979-8-88819-351-8 (paperback).
Subjects: SPORTS & RECREATION / Hunting | HISTORY / United States / State & Local / Middle Atlantic | BIOGRAPHY & AUTOBIOGRAPHY / Sports.

Designed in the USA
0 1 1 2 3 5 8 13 21 34 55

For the Love of Books!

Cover: Based on John James Audubon *Common American Wild Cat* circa 1845 from the American Museum of Natural History.

CONTENTS

Foreword x
Preface ix

    I.   Introduction 1
   II.   The Wild Cat 3
  III.   The Bobcat, or Catamount 6
  IV.   The Big Grey Wild Cat, or
          Canada Lynx 10
   V.   The Blue Mountain Cat 14
  VI.   Mixed Breeds 16
 VII.   Cat Hunting 18
VIII.   Cat Hunters 25

Index 35

ILLUSTRATIONS

"France" Hower . . . . (Frontispiece)
"Clem" Herlacher 4
Emanuel Harman 8
Jesse Logan 11
"Jake" Zimmerman 20
"Phil" Wright 24
C. E. Logue 27
LaRoy Lyman 29
Dr. W. J. McKnight 29
Abe Simcox 29
Sam'l Matter 31
Robert Karstetter 33

FOREWORD.

MUCH has been written about Henry Wharton Shoemaker over the years. While many value his collected myths and legends, others have challenged their authenticity or veracity. As well, Shoemaker's life was full of ebbs and flows and ups and downs. His achievements, on the surface, appear as one of his stories. They seem improbable, if not impossible, but portray a life well-lived and well-intended. While his start in life was surely helped by his upper-class upbringing during the Gilded Age of Manhattan, the ability to collect and spin yarns and connect with so many people was a rare gift. This brief volume regarding the wild cats of Pennsylvania is rich with information about the former feline inhabitants of the Commonwealth. More importantly, it overflows with the stories and lives of the hunters and naturalists who tracked them, whether for sport, financial gain, science, or a desperate meal. What is clear from its pages—Henry Wharton Shoemaker loved the mountains of Northern Appalachia and was enwrapped by the allure of their flora, fauna, and inhabitants, whether pioneers, Natives, or industrialists. Of course, as the editor of this volume, I was initially skeptical of the exploits of the men described in these pages. Knowing Shoemaker's work and reputation, I was suspect of the existence of the men, let alone their exploits. Thus, I set out to research and annotate my findings regarding the individuals mentioned. These footnotes provide further depth and breadth to this brief volume and fortunately build confidence in its content. Alas, nearly all the individuals mentioned in this volume were real men who lived where Shoemaker described. The few exceptions were likely real but current records do not permit confirmation. Some of the individuals in this volume merit deeper exploration, especially John "Trapper" Swoope of Huntingdon. This editor is surely headed to the archive that holds his notes and drawings. Of course, the pictures of some of these men are priceless. They recall a simpler time when a man with a rifle could subsist for decades in a lonely cabin in the woods, at peace with nature. They also recall a time when the fauna were in abundance, before over hunting and industrialization overwhelmed the ecosystems. So, enjoy this time capsule of life on the Allegheny Plateau as told by the "Mark Twain" of Pennsylvania. While this editor is confident the characters herein were real, I cannot speak for their accomplishments, which seem extraordinary, if not impossible. Perhaps there is a bit of embellishment or exaggeration among the facts, but the entertainment value is beyond compare. Enjoy! And as H.W. says, "GIVE THE WILD CATS A CHANCE."

Lawrence Knorr, Ph.D.
April 12, 2025.

PREFACE.

AFTER the widespread research of S. N. Rhoads[1] it might be said that there is little left to write on concerning Pennsylvania wild cats. However, there have been changes in the numbers and the prospects of these most persecuted animals since *Mammals of Pennsylvania and New Jersey* appeared in 1903. In addition to offering a brief for the protection of the lynxes, space will be devoted in the following pages to the noble sport of cat hunting and the bold spirits who took a leading part in the chase in Pennsylvania, past and present. But the main idea of this book is to obtain for the wild cats, now on the verge of extinction, a re-hearing of the trumped-up evidence against them—so that they may get another chance. Let us preserve this picturesque and useful mammal for future generations.

Henry W. SHOEMAKER.
Altoona Tribune Office, February 15, 1916.

---

1. Samuel Nicholson Rhoads (1862–1952) was an ornithologist. His papers are kept at the Historical Society of Haddonfield, New Jersey. He is buried at the Haddonfield Friends Meeting Cemetery in that town. His book *The Mammals of Pennsylvania and New Jersey* was self-published in Philadelphia in 1903.

I.

INTRODUCTION.

WHEN, through villainous bounty laws, the existence of one of the most useful animals in Pennsylvania is threatened, it seems high time for a voice of protest to be raised. Immediately, the question will be asked: what is the use of the wild cat? Its values are manifold. In the mountainous districts, where hunters are few and far between, rabbits—unless kept in check by wild cats—would become so numerous that they would destroy vast numbers of growing trees by eating off their bark. As all good Pennsylvanians aim to aid in the reforestation of the desolated areas in the state—after the forest fire menace has been checked, the wild cat should be preserved to help along the arboreal millennium. In the settled neighborhoods, where farmer boys and city hunters keep rabbits killed off, there is little need for wild cats. And the cats have the common sense to stay away from such localities, though they have on rare occasions come near barnyards or henhouses. Such cats are renegades to their race and should be killed. But the vast majority of wild cats follow out their lives hunting rabbits, rats, mice, shrews, and other vermin. They prey on the rats and mice which destroy the eggs of game birds. They eat much carrion and, as such, are invaluable forest scavengers. They are performing faithfully the duties for which the same God who created us made them to do. If rabbits become scarce, wild cats decrease, just as does the Canada Lynx of the North; bounty laws are unnecessary, wasteful and cruel, a sop thrown by crafty politicians to keep the mountaineer vote in line. If there were no rabbits in the mountains, there would be no wild cats. Note carefully the sections of the state where cats are rare, all for the same cause—lack of food supply, when not wiped out by the mercenary bounty hunters. Those who slaughter wild cats wantonly are false to posterity, unacquainted with natural history and ignorant of the scheme of nature. There is some excuse to hunt wild cats for the sport if no attempt is made to annihilate the species. It provides a grand chase for men and dogs, gives city men a love of the open, and, when the cat escapes, furnishes fun for the cat. The wild cat is fairly valuable as a furbearer; its relative, the Canada Lynx, was much more so, but it is now totally extinct in Pennsylvania, at least the pure race. Therefore, as an aid to sylviculture, as a means of sport, and for its fur, the wild cat deserves protection. Its meat is considered very good. Such men as Dr. C. Hart Merriam[2] and Professor E. Emmons[3] pronounce it most excellent. It was a favorite relish for the old pioneers in the Pennsylvania mountains and the Indians. Another cause for the protection of *Lynx Rufus*. And then there is the sentimental side, which side appeals only to the few. But it is real; animals have rights; they add to the sum total of the beauty and picturesqueness of this world of ours. We have no right to condemn a species to extermination that a Wise Power saw fit to create. It is a presumption on our part. Who gave us such authority?

GIVE THE WILD CATS A CHANCE.

---

2. Clinton Hart Merriam (1855–1942) was a well-known zoologist from New York who died in California. He was known as the "father of mammalogy."

3. Ebeneezer Emmons (1799–1863) was trained in medicine and as a geologist from New York. He was both a professor of chemistry and obstetrics! Emmons was the founder of American Paleozoic stratigraphy and the first discoverer of the primordial fauna in any country.

II.

THE WILD CAT.

WHEN, as a young boy in 1897, the writer first paid a visit to Loganton, "the hunting capital" of Sugar Valley, Clinton County, and was invited to inspect the barber shop trophy room of that prince of Pennsylvania wild cat hunters, Clem F. Herlacher,[4] the most noticeable object in the collection was a long-tailed, cat-like specimen that occupied the place of honor over the central mirror. "That is," said Herlacher, pointing to the trophy, "what the first settlers called a 'wild cat'; in reality, it is the cub of the panther, *felis couguar*. The old-timers often ran across these huge kittens in the woods; they were always blundering into the traps, or their dogs were killing them, and they did resemble 'cats,' with their fluffy fur, broad faces, and long tails. But gradually, the truth dawned on them when they found these 'wild cats' trailing along with mature pantheresses or smaller-sized ones taken from panther nests on rocky ledges. They were not wild cats at all but half-grown or cub panthers. When our forefathers were calling the cub panthers 'wild cats,' they were calling the true, stump-tailed wild cats catamounts, making that designation another absurd mistake. The true wild cat is the bay lynx, whereas the catamount is really the Northern or Canada lynx, always a rare animal in Pennsylvania, and unknown in most of the counties except in the Northern Tier."

At the close of this dissertation, the words of which became indelibly impressed on the writer's mind, Herlacher pointed to a second stuffed animal on a shelf above another of the mirrors. "There," he said, "is a true wild cat—*Lynx Rufus*—a fine specimen; it weighed thirty-five pounds

---

4. Clemens Franklin Herlacher (1856–1937) was born in Loganton, Clinton County, Pennsylvania. He died in Paden City, Wetzel County, West Virginia. He is buried at Greenlawn Memorial Park in nearby New Martinsville. He was the brother of Elmer Ellsworth Herlacher (1862–1929) who was the father of the author's longtime mistress, Hilda Marian Herlacher Petroplos (1895–1979). Thus, Shoemaker was expounding about his mistress's uncle.

"CLEM" HERLACHER, Loganton, Clinton County.
Greatest living Pennsylvania wild cat hunter.

when I killed it two years ago near Captain Green's Trench in Green Gap,[5] down the valley. See, it has a short tail, about six inches, is more distinctly mottled than the panther cub, its fur is shorter and smoother."

The writer then inquired where the panther cub had been obtained. Herlacher replied that he had on two successive years—1892 and 1893—secured panther cubs from a nest in the Panther Rocks, in Black Wolf or Treaster Valley, Mifflin County. He had trailed the old panthers on their regular crossing from Sugar Valley. It was in Treaster Valley that the noble Pennsylvania lion or panther made its last permanent abode in Pennsylvania, the cubs taken by Herlacher being, as far as known, the last panthers born in a wild state in the Keystone Commonwealth. As curios, they were in great demand, but he regretted not having taken them alive. The great hunter had given away all but the one adorning the shelf above the central mirror. Later, it became moth-eaten and was thrown away. Alas! for a priceless natural history specimen.

From the above, it will be plain to the readers of these pages that the original "wild cat" was the panther cub, the wild cat of today is the bay lynx, and the real catamount is the Canada lynx. But the next few chapters will go into these matters more in detail.

Emmanuel Harman,[6] of Mt. Zion, Clinton County, aged 84 years, and many others, have regaled the writer with the story of the wildcat panther-cub blunder of the "pioneer naturalists."

---

5. The story of Captain Green is an embellishment by the author. He and friends Daniel Mark, A. D. Karstetter, and A. W. Zimmerman erected a marble monument to the dubious Captain Green in 1916 (now just off Interstate 80 at the Jersey Shore exit) regarding an event Shoemaker claims happened in 1801, as described in his book *Juniata Memories* in his story "Green Gap." Shoemaker, or one of his storytellers, apparently moved the events of the massacre of Captain Phillips' Rangers twenty years earlier, in 1780, in Bedford County to closer to his home and attributed the events to a Captain Green.

6. Emanuel Harman (1832–1917) was buried in Mount Zion Cemetery in Clinton County, Pennsylvania. According to his death certificate, he was a farmer.

III.

THE BOBCAT, OR CATAMOUNT.

C. W. DICKINSON,[7] experienced hunter and naturalist of Smethport, McKean County, describes the true Pennsylvania wild cat (*Lynx Rufus*), sometimes called the bobcat, and erroneously called the catamount, as follows:

> The size of the average grown wild cat is: Length from nose to base of the tail, 30 inches; tail 4 inches; weight, about 26 pounds. The longest cat I ever saw weighed tipped the scales at just 32 pounds. The wild cat only raises one litter of kittens annually, the time they are born being the 15th or 20th of April. The number of kits in the litter varies from two to five. The weight of a kitten at eight months after birth will be from thirteen to seventeen pounds. It takes them about three years to get their full growth. It is the opinion of many of the old

---

7. Charles Wilson Dickinson is buried at Rose Hill Cemetery in Smethport, McKean County, Pennsylvania.

"C. W. Dickinson, farmer, P. O. Norwich, is a son of Edward H. and Roxie (Comes) Dickinson, the former a native of New Jersey, and the latter of Norwich township, McKean Co., Penn. The father came to McKean County in 1833, and engaged in hunting and trapping, at one time killing fifty-seven deer in twenty-five days; he also killed three elks and twenty bears in McKean County. C. W. Dickinson is the second son of eight children. He was born in Norwich Township, November 10, 1842, and received his education in the common schools of Norwich. July 9, 1861, he entered the United States service, enlisting in Company I, Forty-second Regiment Pennsylvania "Bucktails," and was discharged on account of disability, returning to Norwich September 28 of the same year. He married, November 18, 1873, Miss Estella P. Denison, a daughter of William and Otteline (Carter) Denison, natives of the State of New York, who came to Norwich Township in 1841. Mr. and Mrs. Dickinson are the parents of four children, viz.: Charlie B., Lena E., Carrie A., and Louis H. Mr. Dickinson is one of the wide-awake men of the township, and has been identified with various local offices. He has taken a great interest in the public schools of the township, and, like his father, has a disposition to hunt and trap, having killed about three hundred deer, nine bears, eighteen wolves, and about twenty wildcats, and caught too much small game to mention here." [Source: *History of the Counties of McKean, Elk, Cameron, and Porter, Pennsylvania . . . Volume 1*, J. H. Beers & Co., Published 1890.]

hunters that the cat, as well as the panther, did not like to stay in a locality inhabited by the grey wolf, as the wolf usually roamed about in droves or squads of from two to ten or twelve in a pack. It seems that the cat family was deathly afraid of the wolf family. Their fear was due to the superior numbers of the wolf family traveling together. It was really surprising how fast the cat family increased in this locality after the wolf became extinct. There are three times as many wild cats in McKean County today as there were fifty years ago, notwithstanding they have been hunted hard since the bounty laws were enacted. Yet I do not think there is more than one cat now to where there were three fifteen years ago, while grouse and rabbits, both 'snowshoe' and 'cottontail,' are also decreasing. The wild cat is a great hunter. Naturally, he is a night prowler. He is fond of 'coon, rabbit, groundhog, all kinds of birds that he can catch, and he can capture a mouse as quickly as a house cat. Wild cats are handy with their paws; they have large nails, which are as sharp as needles.

The present range of the wild cat is practically the same as it was when S. N. Rhoads' admirable work on Pennsylvania and New Jersey animals appeared in 1903, which was the entire State of Pennsylvania, except Allegheny, Armstrong, Beaver, Butler, Crawford, Erie, Mercer, and Washington Counties in the west, and Bucks, Chester, Delaware, Montgomery, and Philadelphia Counties in the east, thirteen out of sixty-seven counties, but its numbers are now sadly diminished since Rhoads made his researches. Preying as it does on sickly and weakly game birds, it was a tower of strength in combatting the "grouse disease"[8] and the "quail blight"[9] and also kept in check the ravages of destructive rabbits and other small mammals. In every district where it has been extirpated, the game birds and game animals have decreased with it until it would look like tame or hand-raised game will alone survive the next quarter of a century. The folly of destroying the wolf, fox, and wild cat will not be understood until it is too late. Nature decrees all forms of

---

8. "Grouse disease," primarily referring to strongylosis, is a parasitic infection caused by the Trichostrongylus tenuis worm, affecting red grouse, leading to reduced survival and breeding success.

9. "Quail blight" is not found in any references and may be an invention of the author.

EMANUEL HARMAN, born May 27, 1832.
An authority on the cat family in Central Pennsylvania.

life or none except the domesticated or semi-domesticated specimens of animals and birds.

If the present bounty law, giving $6 for every wild cat's scalp, is continued, few cats will be left in the state by 1921. They are wholly absent from many localities where they were fairly numerous five years ago. They are practically extinct in the Blue Mountains, the Bald Eagle Mountains, and the main chain of the Alleghenies. In northeastern Pennsylvania, a few are taken annually at Blooming Grove Preserve in Pike County; in Clinton County, some are trapped every year in Otzinachson Park—drawn thither by the rabbits and entrails of deer—but these preserves will be responsible for the destruction of all the cats in their respective localities; they will last longest in parts of McKean and Cameron Counties, away from settlements, in the Seven Mountains in Centre and Mifflin Counties, and eastern Clinton County, in the Zimmerman country, unless destroyed by the increasingly frequent forest fires.

There is a great diversity of coloring in specimens of Pennsylvania wild cats. They are mostly of a cinnamon brown color, black striped or spotted on the legs and shading into a white or marbled on the belly. Some are of a rich chestnut brown, beautifully spotted with black, while a few are of a grey drab in color, the black markings resembling bars rather than dots. They usually have a white patch on the ears.

IV.

THE BIG GREY WILD CAT, OR CANADA LYNX.

JOHN G. DAVIS,[10] the old-time woodsman of McElhattan, Clinton County, gives the best description of a mammoth Canada Lynx (*Lynx Canadensis*) killed by John Pluff at Hyner[11] in that county in 1874. Pluff, who was a noted hunter in his day, died in January 1914, in his 74th year. One evening, when Pluff was at supper, he heard a commotion in his barnyard. Taking down his rifle, he hurried out, only to notice a shaggy animal moving about among the feet of his young cattle. Courageously driving the steers into the barn, he came face to face with a gigantic Canada Lynx, or what was called, in northern Pennsylvania, a "Big Grey Wild Cat," or catamount, to distinguish it from the smaller and ruddier Bay Lynx. Aiming for the monster's jugular, Pluff fired, killing the big cat with a single ball. The shot attracted the neighbors, among them Davis, and they gazed with amazement at the giant carcass, the biggest cat killed in those parts since Sam Snyder[12] slew his 10-foot panther on Young Woman's Creek[13] in 1858. The Canada Lynx measured four feet ten inches from the tip of the nose to the root of the tail (the tail measured four inches) and weighed seventy-five pounds. The next day being Thanksgiving, it was supplemented to the turkey feast, and all enjoyed the deliciously flavored white meat more than the conventional "Thanksgiving Bird."

---

10. John G. Davis (1842–1921) was born in New York and died in Jersey Shore, Pennsylvania. He is buried at the Stamm Cemetery in McElhattan, Pennsylvania. He was a Civil War veteran.
11. There are two John Pluffs at Hyner in those days, a father and son. Neither died in 1914 at the age of 74. Perhaps the date of the event of 1874 became confused with the age of the individual. It is more likely the John Pluff of this story was the father (1815–1879) who was a Civil War veteran. The son (1855–1906) was only nineteen at the time of the event.
12. Samuel Snyder (1821–1897) is buried at Linwood Cemetery in McElhattan, Pennsylvania.
13. Young Woman's Creek enters the West Branch of the Susquehanna River near Renovo, Pennsylvania.

THE BIG GREY WILD CAT, OR CANADA LYNX.   11

JESSE LOGAN (1809–1916).
An Indian Hunter of Warren County who killed many wild cats.

This lynx was probably a straggler from the Northern Tier, as none of its kind have been about Hyner since. At the same time, the Canada Lynx has been killed in many parts of Pennsylvania, as far south as the Seven Mountains and Somerset County, some claim, but never frequently. Jesse Logan, Indian hunter of the Cornplanter Reservation in Warren County, who is now 107 years old, says that he cannot recall Canada Lynxes ever having been plentiful in any part of northern Pennsylvania.[14]

Clem Herlacher has killed a number of these animals in Clearfield and Cameron Counties but in widely different localities and on different dates. He describes the Canada Lynx as follows:

> The two most remarkable characters of the Canada Lynx are the beautiful pencils of black hair which ornament the ears, and the perfect hairiness of the soles of the feet, which have no naked spots or tubercles like other species of the feline race. The catamount, which is the true Pennsylvania title for this animal, is of an ashen grey in color, with a ruff of stiff dark hair about its neck and looks 'chuffier' than the common wild cat; it most resembles an Old English Sheep Dog. I know nothing of its domestic habits, though I believe it formerly bred in some of our northern counties. Dr. Merriam says that it has two kittens at a birth. The biggest catamount I ever killed measured, exclusive of the tail, forty inches; the tail measured four inches or an inch shorter than most wild cats. Catamounts were driven into Clinton and Mifflin Counties by forest fires from their northern range but never remained long. I think that the Canada Lynx is now totally extinct in Pennsylvania. It was a fierce fighter, but I have heard of Seneca Indians who tamed it to follow them about like dogs. Among the Pennsylvania Dutch, it was supposed to be endowed with the power to look through opaque bodies; hence the old expression of a person with keen sight being 'lynx-eyed.'

Rhoads records instances of catamounts taken in Cameron, Potter, Columbia, Forest, Lackawanna, Lycoming, McKean, Monroe, Pike,

---

14. Jesse Logan died February 17, 1916. According to Kevin Striver, he was the great-grandson of Chief Shikellamy, grandson of Chief John Logan, and husband of Susan Blacksnake.

Wayne, Somerset, and Tioga Counties. Jesse Harman and son Ed, accompanied by Sam Matter, "California Sam,"[15] a noted trapper, took a catamount at the head of McElhattan Run in Clinton County early in 1903. Out of a dozen cats caught by these hunters that winter, it was the only Canada Lynx. It weighed sixty-five pounds and measured exactly five feet from tip to tip.

---
15. Samuel Matter (1850–1921) (pronounced Motter) was born in Sugar Valley, Clinton County, Pennsylvania, and is buried at Mount Pleasant Cemetery in Rosecrans, Pennsylvania. From the Sugar Valley Historical Society: He was a husband, a father, a farmer, a fisherman, a trapper, and mostly an " adventurer." He lived in the Rosecrans mountains and seemed to be a rather eccentric man. He seldom wore shoes and was often under the watchful eye of law enforcement, although he never was arrested for a crime. He knew his way around the mountains and as many said in the time "he was not afraid of anything". Many embellished "stories" were told of Sam over the years. He got the nickname "California Sam" because he reportedly walked all the way to California carrying his shoes across his shoulder to collect an inheritance from his father—approximately $2,500. He said he never liked to wear shoes because they hurt his feet! "Hip boots" Sam Motter was also known as a sneaky man. He and a friend went fishing one day. The friend did not have much success, but Sam was pulling them in left and right. Sam had a basket to put his fish in and he wore a pair of hip boots. On the way back home, they ran into the fish warden who asked to see the fish they had caught. Sam showed him the basket and the warden said that it was OK. As the warden walked away Sam told his friend that they were lucky. The friend could not understand why until Sam showed him all the fish in the folds of his hip boots. Sam was a great outdoorsman and spent much of his time fishing and hunting. He spent little time with his wife and children. The shot gun that he once owned was given to the Sugar Valley Historical Society by the family of the late Harold "Dutch" Washburn.

V.

THE BLUE MOUNTAIN CAT.

AN animal so widespread in its range as the wild cat doubtless has had many diversified types, even sub-species. Hunted for the most part by unscientific persons, no descriptions have been kept, and all have been classed alike in the bounty records. A few years ago, while in conversation with the venerable artist and nature-lover, C. H. Shearer of Reading,[16] the subject turned to wild cats. "Are you aware," said the old naturalist, "that the wild cats from the Blue Mountains east to the Delaware were vastly different from the cats found in other parts of Pennsylvania? I am not certain of any marked difference between, say, the cats of Potter County and those of Fulton County, except perhaps that they reached the maximum size in the central part of the state, in the Seven Mountains. But in the Blue Mountains and on Penn's Mount, we used to take a cat vastly different from the cats of the Juniata country. In my opinion, the Blue Mountain cat was the 'mountain cat' described by Loskiel.[17] Its coloring, according to that early observer, was 'reddish or orange colored hair, with black streaks.' As a boy, I used to trap many of these cats in Irish Gap and at the head of the Schwartzbach, back of Tuckerton.[18] These cats were short-coupled, compact, rather short-legged, with long, wavy fur, much like the modern pet Angoras in confirmation, except for the short tails. Ten or fifteen-pound cats were big specimens. In the wintertime, they were pale greyish colored, like the Canada Lynx; in summer, they were an orange color, and instead of being dappled were striped like tigers. When I first saw the cats in central Pennsylvania, I was

---

16. Christopher H. Shearer (1846–1926) was a renowned landscape painter from Berks County, Pennsylvania. He was one of the founders of the Reading Public Museum. He is buried in Good Shepherd Cemetery in Muhlenberg Township.

17. George Henry Loskiel (1740–1814) was a Moravian minister who settled near Bethlehem, Pennsylvania. He wrote about the Moravian missions among the Native Americans.

18. Tuckerton is an unincorporated community in Muhlenberg Township, near Temple, Pennsylvania.

struck by the difference—the Juniata cats so ungainly, with higher hind legs than front legs, they were usually so meager looking, and their noses were longer. When I was a boy, before the Civil War, Blue Mountain cats were common in all the hilly regions in Berks, Lancaster, Lebanon, and Lehigh Counties. I have not seen one since about 1870."

The writer at once started on a search for the hide of a Blue Mountain cat, being rewarded by securing a fine hide corresponding exactly to Shearer's descriptions. The hide was of a mature bore cat in its winter coat, which had been killed, according to Paul Weber,[19] the Reading taxidermist, in the Blue Mountains near Millersburg[20] in 1864. In color, it closely resembles a Canada Lynx; its legs are very short. A large stuffed wild cat in the bar room of the hotel at Upper Bern, Berks County,[21] said to have been killed in the Blue Mountains near Shartlesville in 1892, has none of these characteristics. It is a typical Bay Lynx. William Henne,[22] a wild cat hunter of Strausstown, Berks County, declares that for a time, both varieties existed in the Blue Mountains.

---

19. From Morton Montgomery's *Biographies from Historical and Biographical Annals of Berks County*, pg. 577: "Paul Weber, the well-known taxidermist, whose place of business is located at No. 161 Buttonwood Street, Reading, Pa., was born in Saxony, Germany, April 16, 1861, son of Carl and Anistina (Wolf) Weber. Carl Weber came to America prior to 1880. He had followed the trade of a weaver in his native country, but locating in Philadelphia he engaged in butchering, continuing in that line until his retirement. He and his wife now live in Philadelphia, where all of their twelve children, with the exception of Paul of Reading, also reside. Paul Weber received his literary training in the schools of Germany, and while yet a boy studied the art of preserving and mounting birds and animals under Professor Bessler, graduating in the art of taxidermy. On coming to America, he located for a time in Philadelphia, whence he went a short time later to Blackwood, N. J., where he remained about two years, and at the end of that time returned to Philadelphia, establishing himself in business. Here he remained until 1903, when he located in Reading. Mr. Weber is an artist in his line, and it has been said of him that he can mount any animal, "from a mouse to an elephant." Specimens of his wonderful work may be seen in nearly every State in the Union. He mounted a beautiful specimen for President Roosevelt's library, and has done work for Senator Penrose, George F. Baer and others.

Mr. Weber was married in 1889, to Helen Helt, a native of Saxony, Germany, and three children have blessed this union: Charles (deceased), Paul J. and Helen. In religious belief Mr. Weber and his wife are members of the Lutheran Church. In his political views his is independent of party affiliations.

Paul Weber (1861–1943) is buried at Laureldale Cemetery in Tuckerton, Berks County, Pennsylvania.

20. Now Bethel, Berks County, Pennsylvania.

21. There were as many as three hotels at Shartlesville, Upper Bern Township, Berks County. Which one had the cat?

22. There are a few William Hennes from Strausstown. If Shoemaker spoke to this William circa 1914 to 1916, then it would have to be William Jacob Henne (1888–1963). However, it is more likely Shoemaker is quoting an earlier William Henne who hunted when the cats were more plentiful. Thus, this might be William H. Henne (1849–1900) buried in Strausstown.

VI.

MIXED BREEDS.

MIKE SULLIVAN,[23] a very intelligent bar clerk at Johnsonburg, Elk County, called the writer's attention to the length of the tail of a mounted cat in the hotel at that prosperous lumber town.[24] "A great many wild cat hides, taken in Elk, McKean, and Forest Counties, are shipped to a fur dealer in town," said Sullivan, "and I have been struck by the length of their tails. I put a foot rule on this one, and it measured exactly twelve inches. That cat, I am told, weighed forty-one pounds. We have quite a few varieties of cats in these parts. First of all, there is the Canada Lynx, grey in color, with tabs on his ears and hair on the soles of his feet; a big, fierce fellow, often weighing fifty pounds. He has always been a scarce cat; even the Indians say he was never plentiful. Secondly, there is the true wild cat, or bobcat, reddish in color, mottled like a fawn, smaller than the Canadian Lynx, but with a longer tail. Thirdly, there is the tame cat gone wild escaped from lumber camps and the like. Some of these grow very big and, in one or two generations, are brindled and bushy tailed. Many people call them 'coon cats.' Then we have the fourth kind, the mixture, hybrid or mongrel, whatever you call it, between the Canada Lynx and the Wild Cat or Bay Lynx. In my opinion, that cat on yonder shelf is a cross between a lynx and a bobcat. Old hunters tell me that the product of that cross has a longer tail than either lynx or bobcat—a throwback to the type of long ago. There may also be crosses

---

23. This individual could not be found in Elk County, Pennsylvania, and appears to be very knowledgeable for a "bar clerk."
24. Unfortunately, the old hotel in Johnsonburg was torn down in 2021. View at: https://www.smdailypress.com/news/johnsonburg-hotel-torn-down-this-week/article_6bbf9f82-5cf5-11eb-9df5-2375bb88b083.html.

between lynxes and bobcats and tame cats gone wild; it happened in the old country, why not here?"

The above observations, which C. W. Dickinson of Smethport has also advanced, have a considerable element of common sense to them. In deer breeding, there is a tendency to throw back to good-headed or poor-headed ancestors, as the case may be.

In South Carolina, there are frequent cases of palmation in the deer due to some English fallow bucks liberated by planters in the eighteenth century. A cross between two varieties of short-tailed lynxes might provide a longer-tailed type. In other respects the cat in the Johnsonburg house showed an accentuation of characters. Its hind legs were apparently twice the thickness of the front legs and very much longer. It was an unsymmetrical animal. Perhaps much of this was due to faulty taxidermy, but that would not account for the length of the tail. Its color, a darker grey than the true lynx, was almost of a drab hue. It was darker about the head, but there were no regular spots. The Canada Lynx early succumbed to changed conditions in his faunal zone, the forest fire, the clearing, the drained swamp, and the passing of the northern hare, but for a time, his blood will live on in the crossbreed with the more adaptable Bay Lynx. As these long-tailed cats are said to be plentiful in the wilder sections of northwestern Pennsylvania, it may be that this new race will possess the power to endure existing conditions best—though S. N. Rhoads says that such a cross would be infertile.

VII.

CAT HUNTING.

C. W. DICKINSON describes cat hunting in Pennsylvania in the following language:

> Wild cats are hunted with hounds chiefly. If pursued by a fast hound, the wild cat will either go into some rocky ledge or go up a tree, as he can climb a tree as easily as a squirrel can. If a hunter has a good cat dog, it is quite an exciting sport. I know as I have often been on a cat hunt. It is a sport that ought to be preserved.

One of the very best outdoor-life articles that have appeared in a sporting magazine in recent years is J. B. Sansom's contribution entitled: "Cat Hunting: A Real Winter Sport," in the January number of *In the Open*.[25] It describes a thrilling cat hunt in which "coon dogs" were used on A. R. Van Tassel's[26] ranch in Cameron County, not far from

---

25. This article and publication could not be located. The author was likely James Buchanan Samson (1826–1885) who was a newspaperman from Indiana, Pennsylvania. Perhaps Shoemaker came across this old article when it was republished.

26. This is likely the A. R. Van Tassel (1853–1921) buried at Brookville, Jefferson County, Pennsylvania. Shoemaker may have misplaced his ranch in Cameron County, though adjacent to Clearfield County. [From *Twentieth Century History of Clearfield County, Pennsylvania and Representative Citizens*, Chicago Ill.: Swoope, Roland D., Richmond-Arnold Pub. Co., 1911, pgs. 519–520] "A. R. Van Tassel, president of the Union Banking and Trust Company, at Dubois, Pa., having also other important interests at this place, resides on his magnificent stock farm, a tract of 300 acres, situated near DuBois, in Clearfield County, Pa. Mr. Van Tassel has been a resident of DuBois since 1884 but he was born in the city of New York, March 31, 1853, of Holland ancestry. Mr. Van Tassel was educated in the public and in a select school at Brooklyn, N. Y., and when he reached manhood he learned the tanning business and served an apprenticeship to it at Woburn, Mass. Subsequently he established a small tannery of his own, at Boliver, N. Y., which he sold in 1884 and then came to DuBois, where he entered into partnership with a brother and John DuBois & Van Tassel Bros. In the above year A. R. Van Tassel retired from the firm and erected his own tannery which has become one of the large industrial plants of the town, employment being given to from seventy-five to 100 men. This private enterprise, as others in which Mr. Van Tassel is interested, has been of public importance to the place, affording remunerative work to a large body of skilled men, serving to solidify capital here and also to exploit DuBois as a favorable point for business investment. Mr. Van Tassel was one of the organizers

Sinnemahoning. The hounds, which had never previously been used on cats, took to the sport at once, and three cats were secured on the hunt.

A. Phillips,[27] a Lock Haven cat hunter, has used Airedale terriers successfully, securing several fine wild cats by this means on Scootac Run, Clinton County.

William Henne, a noted cat hunter residing at Strausstown, Berks County, trained beagles to trail wild cats in the Blue Mountains when cats were plentiful in that region twenty years ago. One Christmas Eve, his dogs started a wild cat that headed toward the mountain back of Fort Northkill. While passing along an old lumber road, a second cat leaped from a persimmon tree on the back of the unsuspecting Nimrod. A struggle ensued, in which Henne was badly clawed. Eventually, he shook off the cat, which the beagles killed, and, continuing the hunt, secured the second cat at its den on the top of the mountain.

George Potts,[28] of Millersburg, Berks County, hunted wild cats with fox hounds, trained especially for cat hunting, and with considerable success for twenty years after the close of the Civil War. Cat hunting is usually carried on when there is a good "tracking snow."

C. E. Logue[29] states that this winter, he shot four wild cats "ahead of his dogs" in northern Clinton County. This grand sport is little prosecuted in Pennsylvania, most of the cats being trapped, a mean advantage to take of a noble game animal.

Wild cats make delicious eating. Not only the old mountaineers but such discerning naturalists as Dr. Merriam and Prof. Emmons have

---

of the Union Banking and Trust Company, of which he has been president ever since its founding. In 1879 Mr. Van Tassel was married first to Miss Jennie Thomas, who died in New York. She is survived by one son, Stephen T., who is associated with his father in business. In 1893 Mr. Van Tassel married second, to Miss Alice Henderson, and they have three children, Blanche, Henderson and Lillian. The family home, Hillcrest Farm, is one of the largest and most valuable stock farms in Clearfield County. Mr. Van Tassel gives special attention here to the breeding of Morgan horses. He has exhibited at numerous fairs and stock shows and has won innumerable blue ribbons and cups, the latest triumph in this line being one of his stud, Bob Morgan, won a blue ribbon at the Madison Square Garden exhibition, in 1910. The new residence erected by Mr. Van Tassel, on Hillcrest Farm, is beautifully located and is equipped with all modern comforts and conveniences. Mr. Van Tassel and family attend the Presbyterian church. A Republican from principle, he gives his political support to that party but has never consented to permit his name to be used for office. He is identified with the Masonic fraternity, and is one of the charter member of the Acorn Club, a social club of DuBois, Pa.

27. This could be Alonzo Phillips (1879–1958) from Lock Haven.

28. This may have been George Potts (1859–1931) who lived in Berks County in Robeson Township. However, there is no connection to Millersburg/Bethel in northern Berks County.

29. Chancey Elnathan Logue (1875–1941) is buried at Gilmore Cemetery in First Fork, Cameron County, Pennsylvania.

"JAKE" ZIMMERMAN.
For Years a Terror to the Bobcats in the White Deer Creek Narrows.

attested to this. As a source of food supply the wild cat deserves protection. Dr. Merriam, in this connection, says: "I have eaten the flesh of the wild cat and can pronounce it excellent. It is white, very tender, and suggested veal more than any other meat with which I am familiar."

The flesh of panthers and catamounts was also highly spoken of by the Pennsylvania backwoodsmen. Lion's meat was regarded as a delicacy by the French soldiers in Algeria. The wild cat is worth hunting, as he is a bold, courageous animal. He will fight to the last breath and has no fear of man or dog.

Last summer, Jake Zimmerman,[30] the celebrated guide and hunter of the "Zimmerman Country" in eastern Clinton County, was followed by a wild cat four miles one night while driving from White Deer Hole Valley to his home in the mountains. It bounded along by the side of his horse and wagon, every few leaps uttering a piercing cry.

Others who have been followed at night by wild cats are Lincoln Conser[31] and W. J. Phillips,[32] of McElhattan, Clinton County, and Reuben Stover[33] and daughter, of Livonia (Stover's), Centre County.

Reverend D. A. Sowers[34] of Lock Haven met a finely spotted wild cat standing on a log in the forest near DuBois during the deer hunting season in 1914. As it appeared to be unafraid, the young hunter promptly ended its life with a well-directed bullet.

According to C. W. Dickinson, the skin of an average Pennsylvania wild cat (if prime) is worth about $1.25. Finely mottled hides bring much higher prices. Mounted specimens sell for about $10 apiece. In the form of rugs they bring from five to eight dollars, according to size and markings.

---

30. Jacob Wren Zimmerman (1853–1940) was buried at Mount Union Cemetery in Carroll, Clinton County, Pennsylvania. He was the son of David A. Zimmerman and Mary Wren. He was a lumberman who worked for Ario Pardee in the White Deer Valley. He was known as a great hunter and fisherman and was widely known as fiddler for mountain dances and a singer of old ballads.

31. Lincoln Allen Conser (1860–1939) is buried at Linwood Cemetery in McElhattan, Pennsylvania.

32. William Jesse Phillips (1863–1942) is buried at Linwood Cemetery in McElhattan, Pennsylvania.

33. Colonel Reuben S. Stover (1837–1910) was the proprietor of the Stover Hotel at Livonia Pa. He was well known to many business & professional men in Lock Haven. His death was due to Bright's disease and heart failure. Mr. Stover had conducted the Stover Hotel for a half a century. He was buried at Livonia Cemetery in Livonia, Centre County. Reuben had two daughters, Caroline and Hattie, so it is not clear which one was stalked by the cat. Stover's brother was Lorenzo Stover. Lorenzo's son Adam "Ad" Stover (1863–1944) was the father of the novelist Herbert Elisha Stover (1888–1963). Hilda Herlacher, a student of the young teacher, Herbert Stover, became the mistress of Henry Shoemaker. It is this connection that likely leads to Stover becoming known as a writer.

34. Nothing could be found about this individual, though a David Adams Sowers (1864–1927), a machinist, lived near Philipsburg, Centre County.

C. H. Eldon,[35] the gifted Williamsport taxidermist, has mounted several thousand Pennsylvania wild cat hides during the past thirty years.

The alleged destructiveness of wild cats, at most a specious argument, is crushed like an eggshell by the testimony of C. E. Logue, gamekeeper at the extensive Otzinachson Park Preserve in northern Clinton County, the "type locality" of the Bay Lynx in Pennsylvania. Within the enclosure of this preserve, which embraces over three thousand acres, several hundred deer are kept. In Mr. Logue's experience he found only one case where wild cats had killed a deer. In this instance, it was a very old deer and may have been found dead by the cats, which dragged it a hundred feet down a hill over the snow and devoured parts of the carcass. Logue has never found evidence that the cats have molested fawns. Fawns have no scent and hence cannot be trailed by cats; the mother deer are well able to care for them. He classes the wild cats as "game hogs" as regards rabbits and rats but capable of causing little trouble to game birds or deer. Yet the management of this same park continues the unscientific methods of the gamekeepers of the Middle Ages, ordering Logue to trap wild cats, foxes, and other useful mammals incessantly. We have progressed in every other branch of human activity except game propagation, and the results show it.

Dr. Warren mentions a cat that followed a young swain in southwestern Pennsylvania, going home from courting his "best girl," finally "treeing" him on a fence and keeping him there until daylight.

"Link" Conser, of Clinton County, had an almost similar experience during his courting days on the ridges south of the "Sugar Valley Hill;" in his case, the cat kept crossing and recrossing the road in front of him, sometimes lying down and purring at him. This kept up until daylight when the cat vanished.

A. R. Sholter reports another case from Weikert, Union County. One night, some years ago, when returning from a call, he had occasion to walk along the tracks of the L&T Railroad. When opposite Chimney Rock, a cat appeared on the ties in front of him, trotting on ahead and sometimes crossing and recrossing the tracks or lying down and rolling.

---

35. Charles H. Eldon (1852–1930) was a successful taxidermist practicing in Williamsport, Pennsylvania. He opened his taxidermy business in Williamsport, Pennsylvania around 1878 and continued on into the twentieth century. He died in 1930 at age 78. He was inducted into the Taxidermy Hall of Fame. Viewed at: https://taxidermyhalloffame.org/charles-h-eldon/.

Dr. Warren[36] wonders if the Pennsylvania wild cat could, by any possibility, be the patron saint of young lovers! In order to show the extent of the slaughter of wild cats in the Keystone State by professional bounty hunters, the following figures, quoted from Dr. Warren's statistics on the subject, may be of interest: In Clinton County, the "cat stronghold," in the years 1885 to 1896, inclusive, 298 bounty claims were paid on wild cats. The largest number in a single year was in 1891 when 91 scalps were brought in. During the first six months of 1914, bounties were paid on the scalps of 62 wild cats in Clinton County. In Clearfield County, during the seven years 1890–1896, bounties were paid on 430 cats. In February 1916, two well-known citizens of Clearfield County killed a wild cat at Crystal Springs, which weighed 46 pounds. It was four feet long. In Centre County, from 1885 to 1895, inclusive, bounties were paid on 252 wild cats. In Potter County, from 1885 to 1896, inclusive, bounties were paid on 264 cat scalps. During January 1916, bounties were paid on the scalps of 45 cats in Potter County. In Sullivan County, from 1886 to 1896, inclusive, bounties were paid on 224 cats. In Huntingdon County, between 1886 and 1896, inclusive, bounties were paid on 127 of these animals. In Franklin County, 1885 to 1896, inclusive, bounties were paid on 196 cats; in Fulton County, during the same period, on 89 cats; and in Cambria County, also between 1885 and 1896, inclusive, on 136 cats. During January 1916, bounties were paid on 221 wild cats in Pennsylvania. And "game," that is, grouse, quail and rabbits, are scarcer now than with all these cats in the woods. When it is considered that in the eighties and nineties, the bounty amounted to only two dollars per cat, and up to 1915 four dollars at most, the toll to be taken at the present bounty of six dollars per cat means extermination. A rogue's march is going on of lazy ne'er-do-wells, idlers, and thugs going to the forests to destroy an animal that the Creator put there for a wise purpose. The presumption of politicians who encourage this in the face of facts is disgusting and discouraging. The writer has no complaint against the man who hunts for food, or fur, or for love of the chase, but he who wipes a species off the face of the earth for a few dollars is earning tainted money and is a traitor to all the higher instincts of his race. The large numbers of starving emaciated wild cats shot in the open woods and fields this winter show that with the scarcity of rabbits, the wild cats themselves will vanish from the face of the earth.

---

36. Benjamin H. Warren (1858–1926) was the first executive secretary for the Pennsylvania Game Commission.

PHIL WRIGHT (at Extreme Right).
Premier Cat Hunter of Southern Pennsylvania.

VIII.

CAT HUNTERS.

Hunters specializing in wild cats were never numerous. Consequently, the roster of celebrated Pennsylvania cat hunters is not a long one. Most cats, as before stated, have been taken in traps, depriving the sport of its real zest. Except in wintertime, when the country is open, the wild cat is difficult to locate. Its coloring blends with rocks and branches; it is quiet and unobtrusive in the extreme.

Dr. B. H. Warren, now Director of the Everhart Museum at Scranton, in his valuable treatise, *Diseases and Enemies of Poultry*, published at Harrisburg in 1897, thus describes the "favorite haunts" of the cats. "These consist," he says, of "forests, rocky ledges, briary thickets, slashings, and bark peelings strewn with decaying logs, fallen trees, and brush piles, grown up with rhododendron (buck laurel)."

At night, the wild cat, like the panther, is much in evidence. A. R. Sholter,[37] a young hunter of Weikert, Union County, describes the nocturnal cries of wild cats answering one another—one on Paddy's Mountain and the other on the White Mountain, the valley of the Karoondinha reverberating with the savage love notes.

Professor Emmons, in describing the panther, says: "Though it will not venture to attack man, yet it will follow his track a great distance; if it is near the evening, it frequently utters a scream which can be heard for miles."

J. W. Zimmerman and others who have been followed at night by wild cats report the same habit, though the cat's cry is much fainter than that of *felis cougar*.

Friends of Clem Herlacher claim for him the distinction of being one of the most famous cat hunters in Pennsylvania in present or former

---

37. Asa Roland Sholter (1887–1967) is buried at Hironimus Union Cemetery in Weikert, Pennsylvania.

times. They aver that he killed fifty Canada Lynxes, at the recital of which record the modest Nimrod "just whittles," taking pains to remind his friends that he has slain half a hundred wild cats, some of them after spirited combats. But in his hunting days in Clearfield County, he surely killed many catamounts.

Ranking high in the list of cat hunters is Sol. Roach,[38] who hails from Windber, Somerset County. Roach is accredited with killing half a hundred wild cats, six of them in one week, at the Bear Rocks, at the head of Beech Creek, in Centre County.

John P. Swoope,[39] the Huntingdon County trapper, has probably taken more cats than any other hunter of the present day in Pennsylvania. He is credited with having trapped at least 500 cats, sometimes thirty in one season.

C. E. Logue, in connection with his duties as gamekeeper of Otzinachson Park in Clinton County, has trapped probably 100 wild cats, some of them large specimens.

Phil Wright enjoys the distinction of having killed more wild cats than any hunter in Southern Pennsylvania. This Nimrod has taken at least 100 cats of various sizes.

W. H. Workinger[40] has taken many cats in the Seven Mountains. This hunter, who resides at Milroy, Mifflin County, in January 1916, caught two cats, one weighing sixty pounds, the smaller one thirty pounds. The big cat measured 37¼ inches from nose to root of tail; the tail measured 6¼ inches.

"France" Hower,[41] who was accidentally shot in a fox trap last summer, was a terror to the wild cats of Jack's Mountain. In his long career as a hunter, he probably killed fifty of these animals.

---

38. An S. J. Roach is buried at Brisbin in Clearfield County. He appears to have a military gravestone from the Civil War era, but no dates are evident.

39. This legendary mountain man was the son of Dr. William and Hannah Swoope and was one of at least eight children. At an early age, the family moved to the old Swoope homestead in Porter Township, between Alexandria and Barree. "Trapper" Swoope was a solitary man and never married. He was a trapper of legendary proportions throughout Central Pennsylvania. For 57 years roamed the wilds of Huntingdon County. He not only trapped but studied and collected wildflowers and herbs. He kept diaries most of his life, but only a few from 1907–1909 have been saved to give unique insight into his solitary life in the mountains of Huntingdon County. Hartslog Heritage has his diaries and photos. Albert M. Rung's *Chronicles of Pennsylvania History* gives this famous trapper much attention. He is buried in an unmarked grave in Alexandria Presbyterian Cemetery.

40. William Henry Workinger (1854–1924) is buried at Woodlawn Cemetery in Milroy, Centre County.

41. Francis Hower (1848–1915) is buried at Westminster Presbyterian Cemetery in Mifflintown, Pennsylvania.

C. E. LOGUE.
The mighty cat hunter of the Sinnemahoning.

George Potts, of Millersburg, Berks County, was for years the leading cat hunter of the Blue Mountains. Between dogs and traps and still hunts, he undoubtedly killed over one hundred Bay Lynxes and Blue Mountain Cats.

Abe Simcox[42] and his son John killed nearly half a hundred cats along the south slope of Sugar Valley Hill in Clinton County.

David A. Zimmerman[43] and his son Jake killed twice that number in eastern Sugar Valley and the White Deer Narrows.

Earl Motz,[44] "the schoolboy hunter" of Woodward, Centre County, has killed many wild cats in the Pine Creek Hollow.

E. N. Woodcock[45] and Laroy Lyman,[46] noted Potter County hunters, undoubtedly killed over one hundred wild cats apiece.

Dr. W. J. McKnight,[47] of Brookville, in his *Pioneer Outline History of Northwestern Pennsylvania*, says: "The catamount is larger than the wild cat. They have been killed in this region six and seven feet long from nose to end of tail. They have tufts on their ear-tips and are often mistaken for panthers.

George Smith,[48] a Washington Township early hunter, who resided in the wilds of Elk County until his death in 1901, killed in this wilderness five hundred catamounts and six hundred wild cats."

Bill Long,[49] the "King Hunter" of Jefferson and Clearfield Counties, who died in 1880, is mentioned by Dr. McKnight as having killed in Pennsylvania five hundred catamounts and two hundred wild cats. His son, Jack Long, who died at his home two miles from DuBois in 1900,

---

42. Private Abraham Simcox (1839–1907) was a Civil War veteran who was buried in the Quiggle Cemetery, Lock Haven, Pennsylvania. His son John Curtin Simcox (1875–1954) is also buried there.

43. David Amm Zimmerman (1883–1946), the son of Jacob Wren Zimmerman, is buried at Linwood Cemetery in McElhattan. Perhaps the author mixed up father and son.

44. Earl Wolf Motz (1893–1984) is buried in Woodward Union Cemetery in Woodward, Centre County. Motz was a retired postmaster of Woodward, where he had worked for 40 years. He was a veteran of World War I, serving in the US Army. He was a member of the Trinity United Methodist Church, Woodward. Mr. Motz was also a member of the VFW of Bellefonte; the Retired Postmasters Association; and P.O.S. of A. of Woodward Camp 357. He was president of the Paradise Hunting Club. Mr. Motz was a former auditor for Haines Township.

45. Eldred Nathaniel Woodcock (1846–1917) is buried at Lymansville Cemetery in Lymansville, Potter County.

46. Laroy Lyman (1821–1886) is buried at Roulette, Potter County, in the John Lyman Cemetery.

47. Dr. William James McKnight (1836–1918) was a physician and state senator. He wrote several books including a history of western Pennsylvania. His older brother was Colonel Amor Archer McKnight (1832–1863) who was killed at the Battle of Chancellorsville. Both are buried in Brookville, Pennsylvania.

48. George Hunter Smith (1827–1901) is buried at Highland Cemetery in Elk County, Pennsylvania.

49. Bill Long (1794–1880) was a renowned hunter. See https://pa-roots.org/data/read.php?4,746188 for more information.

LaROY LYMAN.
Nationally renowned hunter.

Dr. W. J. McKNIGHT.
Physician and author.

Abe Simcox.
Sugar Valley Hill hunter.

killed, according to a statement made by him to Dr. McKnight, "wild cats and catamounts without number."

E. H. Dickinson,[50] pioneer hunter of McKean County, killed a number of Canada Lynxes, or catamounts, during his early days in the Northern Pennsylvania wilderness. He died in 1885, aged 75 years. With his son, C. W. Dickinson, he helped kill his last catamount in November 1867. In commenting upon the Canada Lynx, Dickinson is quoted thus by S. N. Rhoads: "We have a cat in McKean County, yet that is called a lynx because of its size and color. Some of them will weigh as high as forty-four pounds. But they are a darker grey than the lynx. I believe they are a cross between the lynx and the common wild cat."

The true lynx is a silent animal, not given to whining or screaming like the wild cat, except when badly wounded. Rhoads states that the early Swedish settlers on the Delaware called the lynx the "Warglo," or wolf-lynx, and the wild cat the "Kattlo," or cat lynx. Among the Pennsylvania Germans the lynx was called the "Harsh Katz," and the wild cat the "Wild Katz." The French in Clearfield County, in the Loup Run Country, now corrupted into "Loop" Run, who came mostly from Picardy, called the lynx or catamount the *Chat Cervier* and the wild cat the *Chat Savage*.

No list of Pennsylvania cat hunters would be complete without a mention of Sam Matter, better known as 'California Sam." He was left a fortune by an uncle who went to California in 1849. Sam Matter's specialty, as long as the supply of cats lasted on the head of McElhattan Run in Clinton County, was catching these animals alive with his bare hands. His dogs would trail the cats to their dens, where Matter would dig them out and, with deft movements, seize them by the throats. He sold the cats at good prices to zoos, shows, hotels, and fanciers.

Robert Karstetter,[51] of Loganton, Clinton County, often used his coon dogs to trail wild cats with considerable success.

Dan Long, who killed the last wolf in Berks County, in Shubert's Gap, in 1886, killed many wild cats and Blue Mountain cats during his eventful career as a hunter.

---

50. Edward Hall Dickinson (1811–1890) is buried at Norwich Cemetery, Colegrove, Pennsylvania. Shoemaker's date of death is four years earlier, but the birth year matches.
51. Robert Howser Karstetter (1841–1922) is buried at the St. Paul's Evangelical Lutheran Cemetery in Loganton, Clinton County, Pennsylvania.

CAT HUNTERS.

SAM'L MATTER, Mt. Zion, Clinton County.
Better known as "California Sam."
Famed for catching wild cats alive with his bare hands.

In the county records of Berks County, *Lynx Rufus* is classed as a "catamount," and the Blue Mountain cat as "wild cat." During the years 1885 to 1893, inclusive, bounties were paid on thirty catamounts and wild cats in Berks County. Of these, eleven were classed as "catamounts," the heavy type of Bay Lynx. The Canada Lynx has not been observed in Berks County for many years.

The Seneca Indian doctors used the fat, blood and excrement of wild cats as a cure for diverse maladies of mankind, including baldness, gout, falling sickness and shrunken sinews. They recommended coats and leggings of cat fur (worn fur inward) for various aches and pains in bones and joints.

Wild cats will breed in captivity if given a large enclosure but kill their young if they are born in close confinement. A "breeding cage" should contain running water, trees to climb on, and much-dense foliage. It should be wired, of course, on top to prevent the agile animals from climbing out.

Wild cats in captivity prefer as food the entrails of animals and fowls, chicken heads, cow and horse heads, fish heads, berries, potatoes, grass, bugs and grubs, but be sure that they get plenty of fresh water. They often become friendly and playful and will have as much enjoyment out of a ball of catnip as a tame "tabby."

"California Sam" gives these quaint views concerning the Pennsylvania wild cat:

> It appeared to me an opportune time to write a few lines on the wild cat to clear up in the minds of the younger generation some of the stories that have been told to me when but a boy, some hair-raising tales of the monster 'catamount,' 'wild cat,' 'bobcat.' 'Now let me say I live in the southeastern part of Clinton County, Pennsylvania, and in my fifty years of travels in the forest, so well I became acquainted with the cat that I could communicate with an old bore cat. This is what he once told me: 'My mate met with a sad failure when she jumped in Sam Matter's face. Although Matter is only a small man, my spirits dropped out of my long legs when I saw the ease with which he

ROBERT KARSTETTER.
A Veteran Clinton County Cat Hunter.

handled his 80-pound pack, and it occurred to me that my little 25 pounds of nerve and sinew would count little in case of any serious trouble with Mr. Matter. I, therefore, got out of his way.

I wish to say to the younger sportsmen that my breed of cats do not attack men under any circumstances when we can get away. In fact, we do not like men at all, and I have heard old hunters say when talking over their campfire that as many years as they had been in the hills, they never had seen a mean, quarrelsome cat, and they wondered where they kept themselves. We wild cats have no special range but come from the highest peaks to the lowest bottoms in the daytime and sleep in some dense thicket or in some cave or under some rock where the sun does not penetrate. As cool dusk comes on we prowl softly about, looking for lazy snowshoe rabbits or some grouse or field mice. Many an unsuspecting brood or aged drumming cock have I devoured as the light grew dim in the spring evening. It is very amusing to sit and watch an old cock grouse as he swells and walks along his log. And when he has his thoughts full of his sweetheart and begins to drum, I just make three jumps, and then with one stroke, I crush the life and conceit out of him. Of course, squirrels, small birds, and even fish are all acceptable when they are foolish enough to come my way. I am also very fond of the remains of deer or other dead animals when killed by hunters. When I am angry, I don't stand with my ears pitched forward like a horse, nor do I show my teeth and growl. When I get mad, I lay my ears well back, just as any other cat does, and the madder I get, the lower I lay them, producing a snaky expression.

In order to get any large and satisfactory photos of me, you must either tree me or catch me in a trap.

So, I will close my quotation. Oh, how dear to my heart is my old hunting coat, my old shooting coat that has worn me so well, for weeks at a time in all kinds of weather, and if it could talk, many's the tale it would tell!

GIVE THE WILD CATS A CHANCE.

INDEX

Alexandria, Pennsylvania, 26
Alexandria Presbyterian Cemetery, 26
Allegheny County, 7
Allegheny Mountains, 9
Allegheny Plateau, x
Armstrong County, 7

Baer, George F., 15
Bald Eagle Mountains, 9
Barree, Pennsylvania, 26
Bear Rocks, 26
Beaver County, 7
Bedford County, 5
Beech Creek, 26
Bellefonte, Pennsylvania, 28
Berks County, 14–15, 19, 28, 30, 32
Bessler, Professor, 15
Bethel, Pennsylvania, 15, 19, 28 (see also Bethel, Pennsylvania)
Bethlehem, Pennsylvania, 14
Black Wolf Valley, 5
Blacksnake, 12
Blackwood, New Jersey, 15
Blooming Grove Preserve, 9
Blue Mountains, 9, 14–15, 19, 28
Boliver, New York, 18
Brooklyn, New York, 18
Brookville, Pennsylvania, 18, 28
Bucks County, 7
Butler County, 7

California, 2, 13, 30–32
Cambria County, 23
Cameron County, 6, 9, 12, 18, 19
Captain Green's Trench, 5
Captain Phillips' Rangers, 5
Carroll, Pennsylvania, 21
Centre County, 9, 21, 23, 26, 28
Chester County, 7
Chimney Rock, 22
Clearfield County, 12, 18–19, 23, 26, 28, 30
Clinton County, 3-5, 9–10, 12–13, 19, 21–23, 26, 28, 30–33
Colegrove, Pennsylvania, 30
Conser, Lincoln Allen, 21-22
Cornplanter Reservation, 12
Crawford County, 7
Crystal Springs, Pennsylvania, 23

Davis, John G., 10
Delaware County, 7
Delaware River, 15, 30
Denison, Estella P., 6
Denison, Otteline (Carter), 6
Denison, William, 6
Dickinson, Carrie A., 6
Dickinson, Charles Wilson, 6, 17–18, 21, 30
Dickinson, Charlie B., 6
Dickinson, Edward Hall, 6, 30
Dickinson, Lena E., 6
Dickinson, Louis H., 6
Dickinson, Roxie (Comes), 6
DuBois, Pennsylvania, 18–19, 21, 28

Eldon, Charles H., 22
Elk County, 16, 28

Emmons, Ebeneezer, 2, 19, 25
Everhart Museum, 25
Erie County, 7

Forest County, 12, 16
Fort Northkill, 19
Franklin County, 23
Fulton County, 14, 23

Good Shepherd Cemetery, 14
Green, Captain, 5
Green Gap, 5
Greenlawn Memorial Park, 3

Haddonfield, New Jersey, xi
Haddonfield Friends Meeting Cemetery, xi
Haines Township, Centre County, 28
Harman, Ed, 13
Harman, Emanuel, 5, 8
Harman, Jesse, 13
Harrisburg, Pennsylvania, 25
Hartslog Heritage, 26
Helt, Helen, 15
Henne, William H., 15, 19
Henne, William Jacob, 15
Herlacher, Clemens Franklin "Clem," 3–5, 12, 21, 25
Herlacher, Elmer Ellsworth, 3
Herlacher, Hilda, 3, 21 (see also Hilda Marian Herlacher Petroplos)
Highland Cemetery, 28
Hironimus Union Cemetery, 25
Hower, Francis "France," frontispiece, 26
Huntingdon County, ix, 23, 26
Hyner, Pennsylvania, 10, 12

Indiana, Pennsylvania, 18

Interstate 80, 5
Irish Gap, 14

Jack's Mountain, 26
Jefferson County, 18, 28
Jersey Shore, Pennsylvania, 5
John Lyman Cemetery, 28
Johnsonburg, Pennsylvania, 16–17
Juniata River, 14–15

Karoondinha, 25
Karstetter, A. D., 5
Karstetter, Robert Howser, 30, 33

L&T Railroad, 22
Lackawanna County, 12
Lancaster County, 15
Laureldale Cemetery, 15
Lebanon County, 15
Lehigh County, 15
Linwood Cemetery, 10, 21, 28
Livonia Cemetery, 21
Livonia, Pennsylvania, 21
Lock Haven, Pennsylvania, 19, 21, 28
Logan, Jesse, 11–12
Logan, John, 12
Loganton, Pennsylvania, 3–4, 30
Logue, Chancey Elnathan, 19, 22, 26–27
Long, Bill, 28
Long, Dan, 30
Long, Jack, 28
Loskiel, George Henry, 14
Loup Run Country, 30
Lycoming County, 12
Lyman, LaRoy, 28–29

Lymansville Cemetery, 28
Lymansville, Pennsylvania, 28

Manhattan, New York, ix
Mark, Daniel, 5
Matter, Samuel, 13, 30–32, 34
McElhattan, Pennsylvania, 10, 21, 28
McElhattan Run, 30
McKean County, 6–7, 9, 12, 16, 30
McKnight, Amor Archer, 28
McKnight, William James, 28-30
Mercer County, 7
Merriam, Clinton Hart, 2, 12, 19, 21
Mifflin County, 5, 9, 12, 26
Mifflintown, Pennsylvania, 26
Millersburg, Pennsylvania, 15, 19, 28 (see also Bethel, Pennsylvania)
Milroy, Pennsylvania, 26
Monroe County, 12
Montgomery County, 7
Montgomery, Morton, 15
Motz, Earl Wolf, 28
Mount Pleasant Cemetery, 13
Mount Zion, Pennsylvania, 5, 31
Mount Zion Cemetery, 5
Muhlenberg Township, Berks County, 14

Native Americans, 14
New Jersey, xi, 6–7
New York, 2, 6, 10, 19
New York city, 18
Northern Appalachia, ix
Northern Tier, 3, 12
Norwich, Pennsylvania, 6
Norwich Cemetery, 30
New Martinsville, West Virginia, 3

Otzinachson Park, 9, 22, 26

Paden City, Wetzel County, West Virginia, 3
Paddy's Mountain, 25
Panther Rocks, 5
Paradise Hunting Club, 28
Pardee, Ario, 21
Penn's Mount, 14
Pennsylvania "Bucktails," 6
Pennsylvania Dutch/Germans, 12, 30
Pennsylvania Game Commission, 23
Penrose, Senator, 15
Petroplos, Hilda Marian Herlacher, 3, 21 (see also Hilda Herlacher)
Philadelphia, Pennsylvania, xi, 15
Philadelphia County, Pennsylvania, 7
Philipsburg, Pennsylvania, 21
Phillips, Alonzo, 19
Phillips, William Jesse, 21
Pike County, 9, 12
Pluff, John, 10
Porter Township, Huntingdon County, 26
P.O.S. of A. of Woodward Camp 357, 28
Potter County, 12, 14, 23, 28
Potts, George, 19, 28

Reading, Pennsylvania, 14–15
Reading Public Museum, 14
Renovo, Pennsylvania, 10
Rhoads, Samuel Nicholson, xi, 7, 12, 17, 30
Roach, Solomon J., 26
Robeson Township, Berks County, 19
Roosevelt, Theodore, 15
Rose Hill Cemetery, 6
Rosecrans, Pennsylvania, 13
Roulette, Pennsylvania, 28

Rung, Albert M., 26

St. Paul's Evangelical Lutheran Cemetery, 30
Samson, James Buchanan, 18
Schwartzbach Creek, 14
Scootac Run, 19
Scranton, Pennsylvania, 25
Seneca Indians, 12, 32
Seven Mountains, 9, 12, 14, 26
Shartlesville, Pennsylvania, 15
Shearer, Christopher H., 14–15
Shikellamy, 12
Sholter, Asa Roland, 22, 25
Shubert's Gap, 30
Simcox, Abraham, 28–29
Simcox, John Curtin, 28
Sinnemahoning, Pennsylvania, 19, 27
Smethport, Pennsylvania, 6, 17
Smith, George Hunter, 28
Snyder, Samuel, 10
Somerset County, 12–13, 26
South Carolina, 17
Sowers, Reverend D. A., 21
Sowers, David Adams, 21
Stamm Cemetery, 10
Stover, Adam, 21
Stover, Caroline, 21
Stover, Hattie, 21
Stover, Herbert Elisha, 21
Stover Hotel, 21
Stover, Lorenzo, 21
Stover, Reuben S., 21
Strausstown, Pennsylvania, 15, 19
Striver, Kevin, 12
Sugar Valley, 3, 5, 13, 28

Sugar Valley Hill; 22, 28–29
Sugar Valley Historical Society, 13
Sullivan County, 23
Sullivan, Mike, 16
Susquehanna River, 10
Swoope, Hannah, 26
Swoope, John P. "Trapper," ix, 16, 26
Swoope, Roland D., 18
Swoope, William, 26

Taxidermy Hall of Fame, 22
Temple, Pennsylvania, 14
Tioga County, 13
Treaster Valley, 5
Tuckerton, Pennsylvania, 14–15

Union County, 22, 25
Upper Bern Township, Berks County, 15
Van Tassel, A. R., 18-19

Warren, Benjamin H., 22–23, 25
Warren County, 11, 12
Washburn, Harold "Dutch," 13
Washington County, 7
Washington Township, Elk County, 28
Wayne County, 13
Weber, Anistina (Wolf), 15
Weber, Carl, 15
Weber, Charles, 15
Weber, Helen, 15
Weber, Paul, 15
Weber, Paul J., 15
Weikert, Pennsylvania, 22, 25
West Branch, 10
Westminster Presbyterian Cemetery, 26

White Deer Creek Narrows, 20
White Deer Hole Valley, 21
White Deer Narrows, 28
White Mountain, 25
Williamsport, Pennsylvania, 22
Woburn, Massachusetts, 18
Woodcock, Eldred Nathaniel, 28
Woodlawn Cemetery, 26
Woodward, Pennsylvania, 28
Woodward Union Cemetery, 28
Workinger, William Henry, 26
Wren, Mary, 21
Wright, "Phil," 24, 26

Young Woman's Creek, 10

Zimmerman, A.W., 5
Zimmerman, David Amm, 21, 28
Zimmerman, Jacob Wren "Jake," 20–21, 28
Zimmerman country, 9, 21

www.ingramcontent.com/pod-product-compliance
Lightning Source LLC
Chambersburg PA
CBHW011802040426
42449CB00016B/3468